Let's Begin!

To Parents: It's important for children to name objects before learning the alphabet. Point to each illustration and ask, "What is this?" If it's right, be sure to praise your child by saying something like, "You're right! That is a green car."

 Here are five very different things. Let's point at each one and say its name.

ALPHABET

A
APPLE

B
BEAR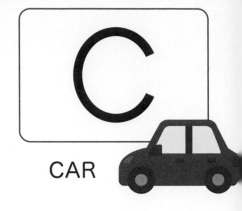

C
CAR

G
GORILLA

H
HIPPO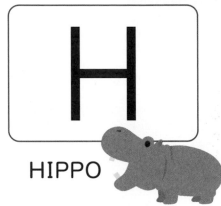

I
ICE CREAM

M
MONKEY

N
NOSE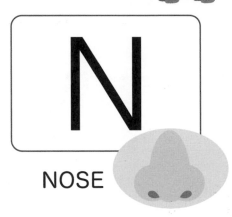

O
OCTOPUS

S
STAR

T
TRAIN

U
UMBRELLA

Y
YACHT

Z
ZEBRA

D

DOG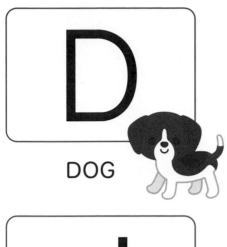

E

ELEPHANT

F

FROG

J

JAM

K

KOALA

L

LION

P

PIG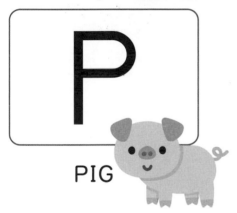

Q

QUEEN

R

RABBIT

V

VIOLIN

W

WHALE

X

XYLOPHONE

Trace the Letter A

To Parents: Trace the letter with your finger, following the numbers and arrows. Hold your child's finger and help them trace the letter. Encourage them to color the apple, too!

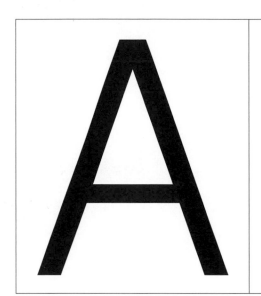 Trace the A and say "A."

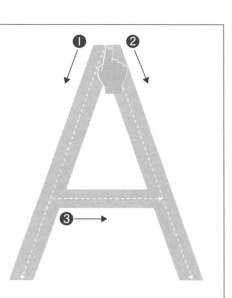

AIRPLANE

APPLE

 Color the APPLE.

A is for APPLE.

Find the Letter A

To Parents: Point to the picture of the airplane on the previous page and say "airplane." Then, engage your child by asking, "Can you find an airplane?"

Find the three airplanes in the picture. Then, find the letter A.

A is for AIRPLANE.

6

Trace the Letter B

To Parents: Trace the letter with your finger, following the numbers and arrows. Hold your child's finger and help them trace the letter. Ask them what color the banana is. Then, encourage your child to finish coloring the banana.

  Trace the B and say "B."

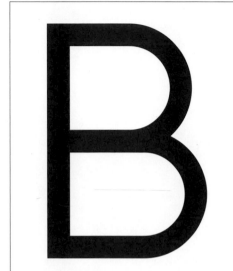 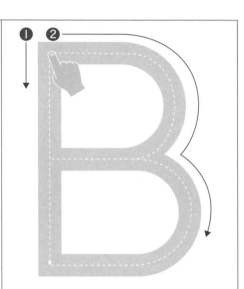

BEAR

BANANA

 Color the BANANA.

B is for BANANA.

Find the Letter B

To Parents: Cut along the solid gray line and fold up from the dotted line. Have your child say "good night" to the bear as they fold and unfold the page. Share with them that "bed" and "blanket" are words that begin with B.

  Cover this bear with his blanket. Then, find the letter B on the bed.

B is for BEAR.

Fold up

Fold the page

How to Play

✂ Parents: Cut along the gray line for your child.

Trace the Letter C

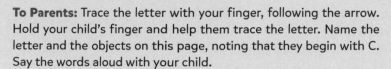

To Parents: Trace the letter with your finger, following the arrow. Hold your child's finger and help them trace the letter. Name the letter and the objects on this page, noting that they begin with C. Say the words aloud with your child.

  Trace the C and say "C."

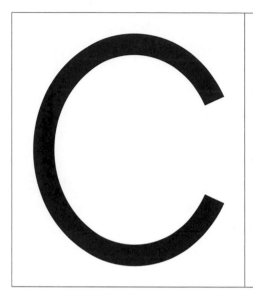 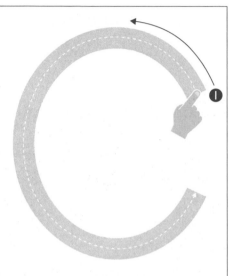

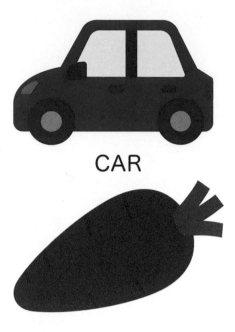

CAR

CARROT

Color the CARROT.

C is for CARROT.

Find the Letter C

To Parents: Cut along the solid gray lines and fold along the dotted line to make a car. Then, have your child move the car along the road while saying "C is for car."

Sticker
Good job!

 Move the car along the line from ➡ to ➡ while saying "C." Then, find the letter C in the picture.

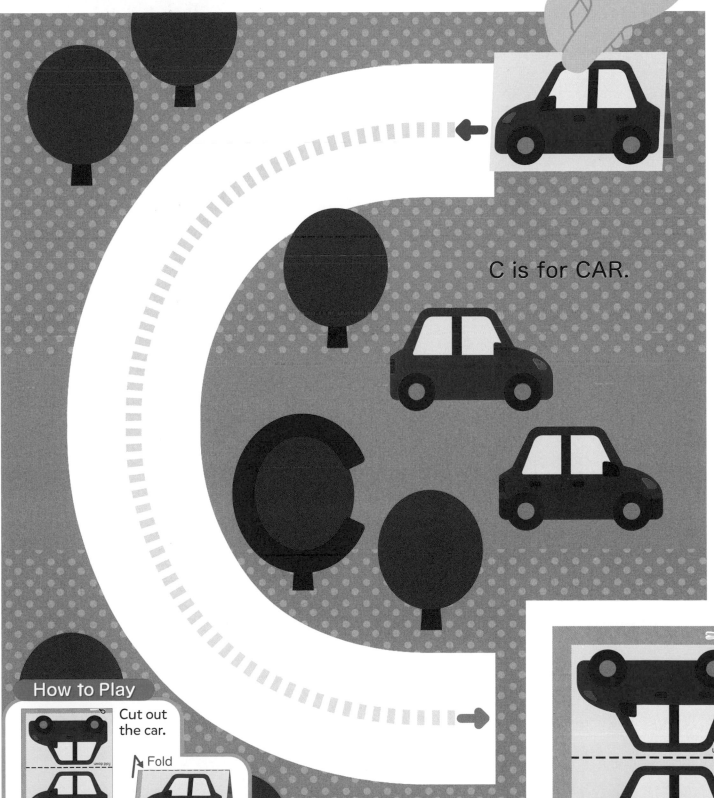

C is for CAR.

How to Play

Cut out the car.

Fold

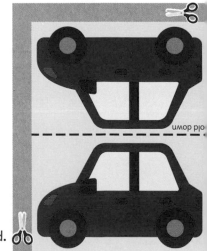

Parents: Cut out the car for your child. ✂

Trace the Letter D

To Parents: Trace the letter with your finger, following the numbers and arrows. Hold your child's finger and help them trace the letter. It's fine if your child does not trace the letter perfectly. It's more important to familiarize your little one with the alphabet.

  Trace the D and say "D."

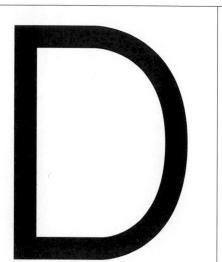 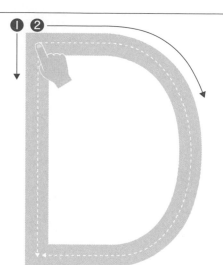

DOG

DOLPHIN

 Color the DOLPHIN.

D is for DOLPHIN.

Find the Letter D

To Parents: This activity focuses on observation skills. Ask your child to point to their favorite dog. Then, ask if they can find the same dog elsewhere. Finally, ask them to point to and then connect the pair.

Sticker
Good job!

 Draw a line to connect the matching dogs.
Then, find the letter D in the picture.

D is for DOG.

example

Sticker

Good job!

Trace the Letter E

To Parents: Trace the letter with your finger, following the numbers and arrows. Hold your child's finger and help them trace the letter. Together, say "E is for elephant." Ask your child what kind of sound an elephant makes. Then, do your best elephant impression!

  Trace the E and say "E."

EGG

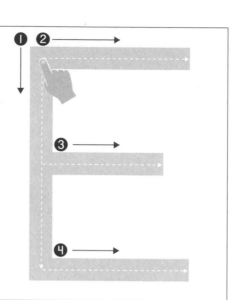

ELEPHANT

Color the ELEPHANT.

E is for ELEPHANT.

Find the Letter E

To Parents: Cut along the solid gray line. Then, fold and crease along the dotted lines. Have your child fold and unfold the page while saying "whole eggs, cracked eggs, egg begins with E."

 Fold and unfold the page. Then, find the letter E in the picture.

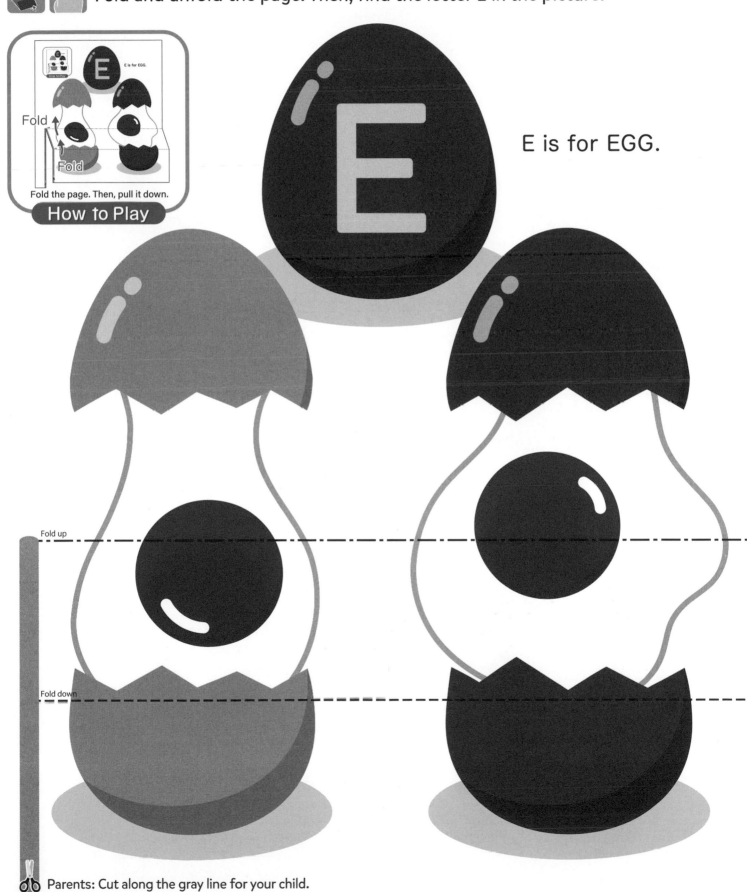

How to Play

E is for EGG.

Fold up

Fold down

 Parents: Cut along the gray line for your child.

Trace the Letter F

To Parents: Trace the letter with your finger, following the numbers and arrows. Hold your child's finger and help them trace the letter. Then, ask your child to name the flowers' colors. Encourage them to choose crayons that match the inside circle of each flower.

 Trace the F and say "F."

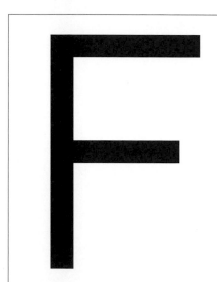

FROG

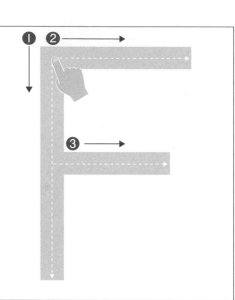

FLOWER

 Color the FLOWERS.

F is for FLOWER.

Find the Letter F

To Parents: This activity focuses on observation skills. Ask your child to point to a frog. Ask them to drag a finger from one frog to the next to make a path through the maze.

Use your finger to connect all the frogs from ➡ to ➡. Say "frog" each time you pass one. Then, find the letter F in the picture.

F is for FROG.

16

Trace the Letter G

To Parents: Trace the letter with your finger, following the numbers and arrows. Hold your child's finger and help them trace the letter. Encourage your child to finish coloring the grapes purple. Say "G is for grapes," and pretend to eat them!

 Trace the G and say "G."

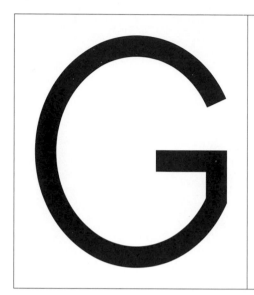 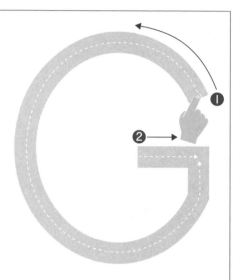

GORILLA

GRAPES

Color the GRAPES.

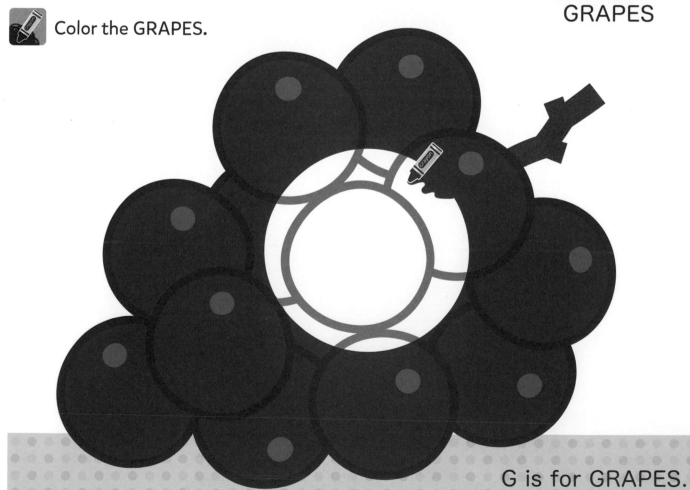

G is for GRAPES.

Find the Letter G

To Parents: This activity focuses on your child's ability to express themselves. Encourage your child to imitate a gorilla by making a deep "hoo-hoo" sound.

 Make the "hoo-hoo" sound a gorilla makes. Then, find the letter G.

G is for GORILLA.

Trace the Letter H

To Parents: Trace the letter with your finger, following the numbers and arrows. Hold your child's finger and help them trace the letter. Ask your child to point to each heart and say what color it is. Then, ask them to choose crayons that match the color of each heart.

Trace the H and say "H."

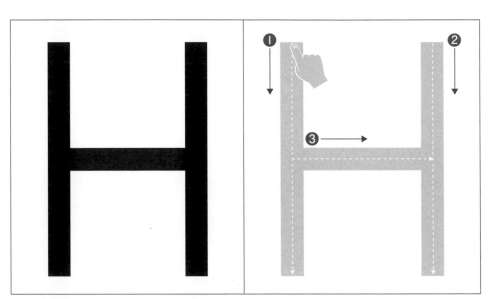

HIPPO

HEART

Color the HEARTS.

H is for HEART.

Find the Letter H

To Parents: Encourage your child to trace the shape of each animal and the shape of the shadow with their finger. Then ask, "Which animal matches this shadow?"

Sticker
Good job!

 Point to the picture that matches the shadow. Then, find the letter H.

H is for HIPPO.

Trace the Letter I

To Parents: Trace the letter with your finger, following the numbers and arrows. Hold your child's finger and help them trace the letter. Ask your child what color the grass on the island is. Then say "I is for island." Ask your child to point to the animals and name them.

  Trace the I and say "I."

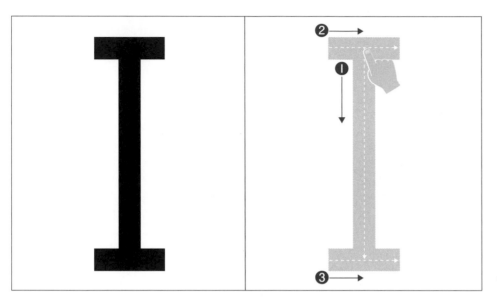

ICE CREAM

ISLAND

Color the ISLAND.

I is for ISLAND.

Find the Letter I

To Parents: Encourage your child to add ice cream stickers to the empty cone in any order they choose. When they are done, say "It looks delicious!"

  Put ice cream stickers on the child's cone. Then, find the letter I.

sticker

sticker

sticker

I is for ICE CREAM.

example

I is for ICE CREAM.

Trace the Letter J

To Parents: Trace the letter with your finger, following the arrow. Hold your child's finger and help them trace the letter. Then, ask your child to name the jam's color. Give them a red crayon so they can spread more jam on the bread. It's fine if they spread the jam outside the bread!

  Trace the J and say "J."

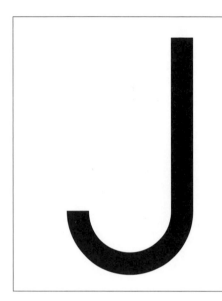
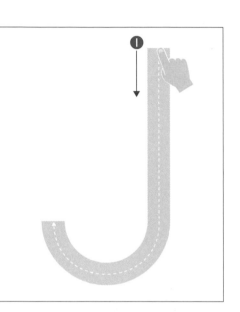

JUICE

JAM

Color the JAM.

J is for JAM.

Find the Letter J

Sticker
Good job!

 Draw juice in the blender. Push the button and pretend to turn it on! Then, find the letter J on the blender.

J is for JUICE.

example

example

Trace the Letter K

To Parents: Trace the letter with your finger, following the numbers and arrows. Hold your child's finger and help them trace the letter. After saying "K is for kangaroo," ask your child what is in the kangaroo's pouch.

  Trace the K and say "K."

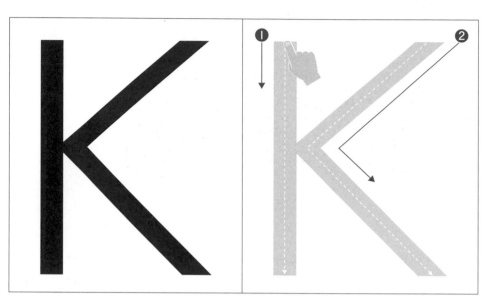

KOALA

 Color the KANGAROO.

KANGAROO

K is for KANGAROO.

Find the Letter K

To Parents: Cut out the koalas along the solid gray lines. Then, give them to your child. Apply glue where it says "glue" and let them place the koalas in the boxes on the tree. This activity helps build fine motor skills.

  Place the koalas in the tree. Then, find the letter K.

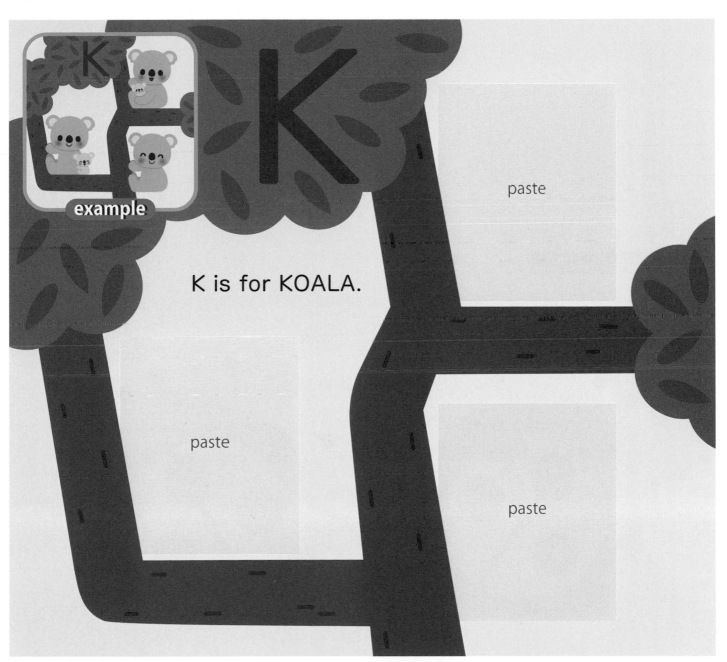

example

K is for KOALA.

paste

paste

paste

Parents: Cut out the koalas for your child.

Trace the Letter L

To Parents: Trace the letter with your finger, following the arrow. Hold your child's finger and help them trace the letter. Say, "The lovely ladybugs are dancing." After your child finishes coloring, ask them to dance with you!

 Trace the L and say "L."

LION

LADYBUG

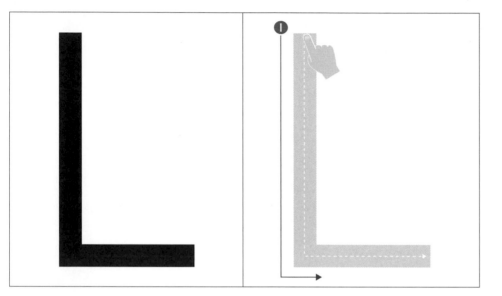

 Color the LADYBUGS.

L is for LADYBUG.

glue

glue

glue

Find the Letter L

To Parents: This activity builds creativity. Encourage your child to draw a mane on the lion. Let them draw freely—it doesn't need to look like the example. Be sure to tell your little one, "Well done!"

  Draw a mane on the lion. Then, find the letter L.

L is for LION.

example

Trace the Letter M

To Parents: Trace the letter with your finger, following the numbers and arrows. Hold your child's finger and help them trace the letter. After saying "M is for mountain," talk about the way the letter M looks like two little mountains.

 Trace the M and say "M."

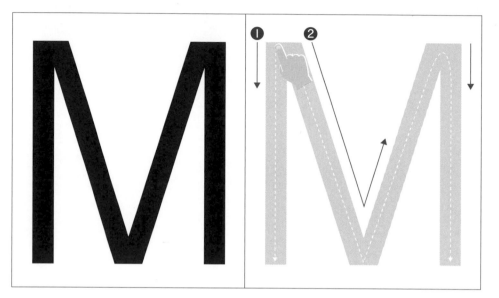

MONKEY

MOUNTAIN

 Color the MOUNTAIN.

M is for MOUNTAIN.

Find the Letter M

To Parents: Encourage your child to place the monkey stickers provided anywhere they would like on the page. Count them together: "One monkey, two monkeys . . ."

  Put the monkey stickers on the tree. Find the letter M.

M is for MONKEY.

example

M

Trace the Letter N

To Parents: Trace the letter with your finger, following the numbers and arrows. Hold your child's finger and help them trace the letter. After saying "N is for night," give your child a blue crayon. As they finish coloring the night sky, ask your child what they say when they go to bed.

  Trace the N and say "N."

 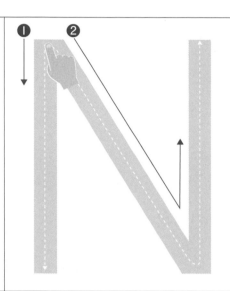

NOSE

NIGHT

 Color the NIGHT sky.

N is for NIGHT.

Find the Letter N

To Parents: Give your child the stickers of animal noses provided. Ask, "Whose nose is this?" and allow them to point and then place each sticker on the animal it matches.

  Put the nose stickers on each animal's face. Then, find the letter N.

N is for NOSE.

Sticker

Good job!

Trace the Letter O

To Parents: Trace the letter with your finger, following the arrow. Hold your child's finger and help them trace the letter. After your child finishes coloring the orange, ask them to help you find more orange objects in your house.

 Trace the O and say "O."

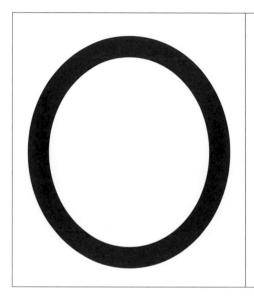
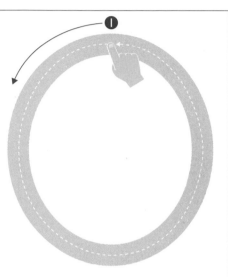

OCTOPUS

ORANGE

 Color the ORANGE.

O is for ORANGE.

Find the Letter O

To Parents: Cut along the solid gray line. Help your child fold and crease along the dotted lines. Encourage them to say "octopus." Then, have them fold the page and say "balloon." Prompt them to fold and unfold the page while saying what they see.

Sticker

Good job!

  What does the octopus become when you fold and unfold the page? Find the letter O in the picture.

Fold

Fold

Fold the page. Then, pull It down.

How to Play

Fold up

O is for OCTOPUS.

Fold down

34

Good job!
Sticker

Trace the Letter P

To Parents: Trace the letter with your finger, following the numbers and arrows. Hold your child's finger and help them trace the letter. After saying, "P is for pig," ask, "Can you oink like a pig?"

  Trace the P and say "P."

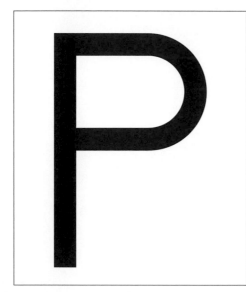
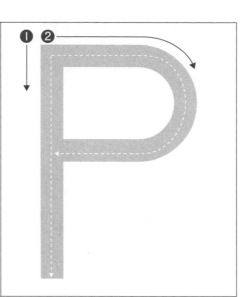

PIG

PINEAPPLE

Color the PINEAPPLE.

P is for PINEAPPLE.

Find the Letter P

To Parents: Point to the picture of the pig on the previous page and say "pig." If the exercise below is too difficult, prompt your child to point to the pig's curly tail before they search for pigs in the picture.

Sticker
Good job!

 Find four pigs. Then, find the letter P.

P is for PIG.

Trace the Letter Q

To Parents: Trace the letter with your finger, following the numbers and arrows. Hold your child's finger and help them trace the letter. In this activity, your child will practice coloring smaller areas than previous pages. When your child is done, compliment them for trying to stay within the white circle on the quilt!

  Trace the Q and say "Q."

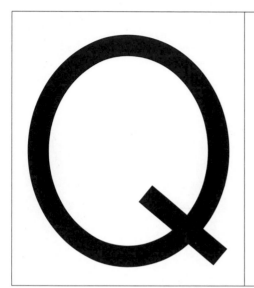

QUEEN

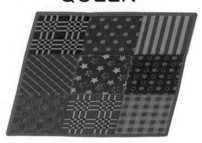

QUILT

 Color the QUILT.

Q is for QUILT.

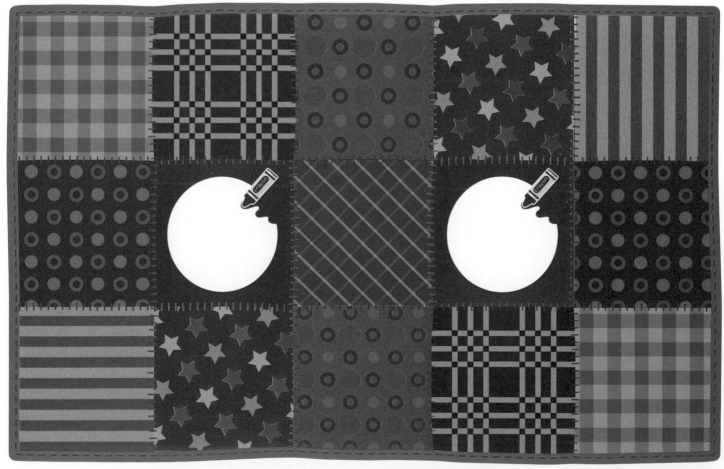

Find the Letter Q

To Parents: Give your child the stickers provided and name the different shapes. Have them decorate and color the queen's dress.

  Put stickers on the queen's dress. Then, find the letter Q.

example

Q is for QUEEN.

Sticker
Good job!

Trace the Letter R

To Parents: Trace the letter with your finger, following the numbers and arrows. Hold your child's finger and help them trace the letter. Tell your child that you will color one rose while they color the other one. Your participation will help motivate your child.

 Trace the R and say "R."

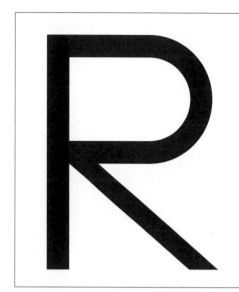
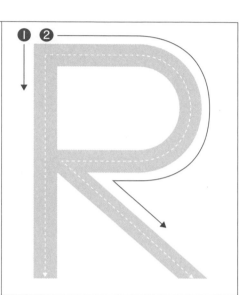

RABBIT

ROSE

Color the ROSES.

R is for ROSE.

Find the Letter R

To Parents: Help your child cut along the solid gray lines. Ask them to add glue to the ears and stick them on the rabbit illustration. Let your child bend and flap the ears!

Sticker
Good job!

 Place the rabbit's floppy ears on its head. Then, find the letter R.

How to Play

Paste

paste   paste

R is for RABBIT.

R

Parents: Cut out the rabbit ears for your child.

Trace the Letter S

To Parents: Trace the letter with your finger, following the arrow. Hold your child's finger and help them trace the letter. Ask them to color the stars. Then, encourage them to draw a smiling face on each star. You can mention that smile begins with S!

  Trace the S and say "S."

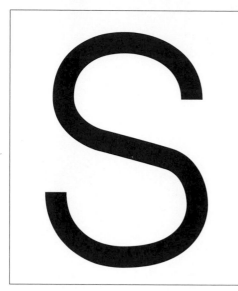

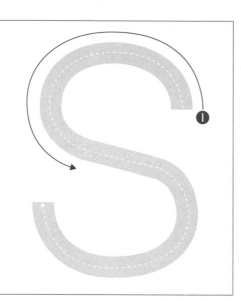

SHEEP

STAR

 Color the STARS.

S is for STAR.

glue

glue

Find the Letter S

To Parents: This activity focuses on creativity and handwriting. Have your child draw one or two squiggles in the shape of a letter S. It's fine if none of the squiggles look like an S. Then, your child can fill in the sheep with lines and dots.

  Draw wool on the sheep. Then, find the letter S.

example

example

S is for SHEEP.

Trace the Letter T

To Parents: Trace the letter with your finger, following the numbers and arrows. Hold your child's finger and help them trace the letter. After they have traced the letter and colored the picture, praise your child for the effort they've put in.

  Trace the T and say "T."

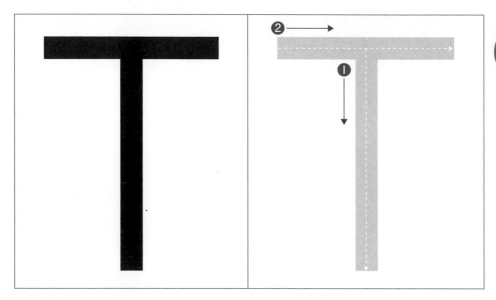

TRAIN

TOMATO

 Color the TOMATO.

T is for TOMATO.

Find the Letter T

To Parents: Cut along the solid gray lines and fold along the dotted line to make the train. Have your child move the train along the track while saying "choo-choo train."

Move the train along the path from ➡ to ➡. Then, find the letter T.

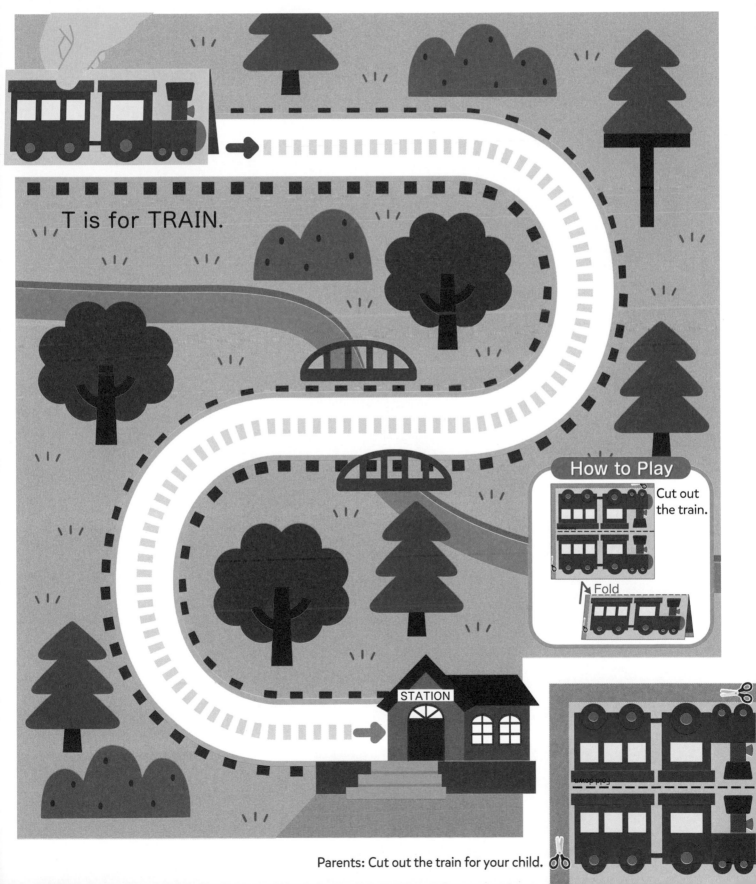

T is for TRAIN.

STATION

How to Play

Cut out the train.

Fold

Parents: Cut out the train for your child.

Sticker
Good job!

Trace the Letter U

To Parents: Trace the letter with your finger, following the arrow. Hold your child's finger and help them trace the letter. Ask your child to find a shape on the unicorn. Ask them what it is. If that is too difficult, draw a heart for them and tell them what it is.

  Trace the U and say "U."

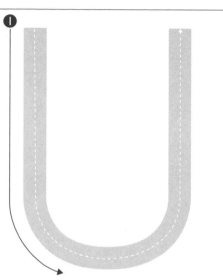

UMBRELLA

UNICORN

 Color the UNICORN.

U is for UNICORN.

Find the Letter U

To Parents: Ask your child to point to one umbrella. Can they find the matching umbrella? If not, point out some similar details, like colors or patterns. Then, ask your child again to point out matching pairs.

 Draw lines to connect each pair of matching umbrellas. Then, find the letter U.

example

U is for UMBRELLA.

Trace the Letter V

To Parents: Ask your child to color the violin. When your child has finished coloring, say "V is for violin" and draw your child's attention to the picture. Then, pretend to play one!

 Trace the V and say "V."

VEGETABLES

VIOLIN

 Color the VIOLIN.

V is for VIOLIN.

Find the Letter V

To Parents: This activity will help your child begin to see part of something and then recognize the whole thing. Begin by naming each vegetable together.

Sticker
Good job!

 Draw a line between each *part* shown in a circle below and the vegetable that it's *part of* on the plate. Then, find the letter V.

V is for VEGETABLES.

example

Trace the Letter W

To Parents: This activity allows your child to practice coloring shapes that are not round. After your little one colors the whale, praise them by saying "good job" or "well done!"

  Trace the W and say "W."

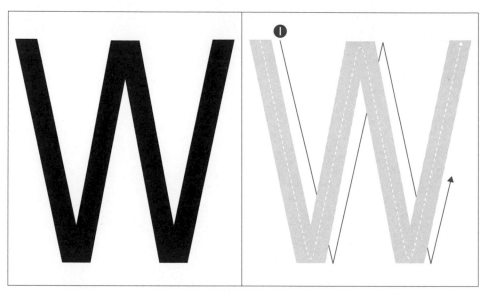

WATERMELON

WHALE

 Color the WHALE.

W is for WHALE.

Find the Letter W

To Parents: Cut along the solid gray line and crease along the dotted lines. Have your child pretend to chop the watermelon in half! Encourage them to fold the paper and say "one whole watermelon." Then, unfold it and say "two halves."

  Fold and unfold the watermelon. Then, find the letter W.

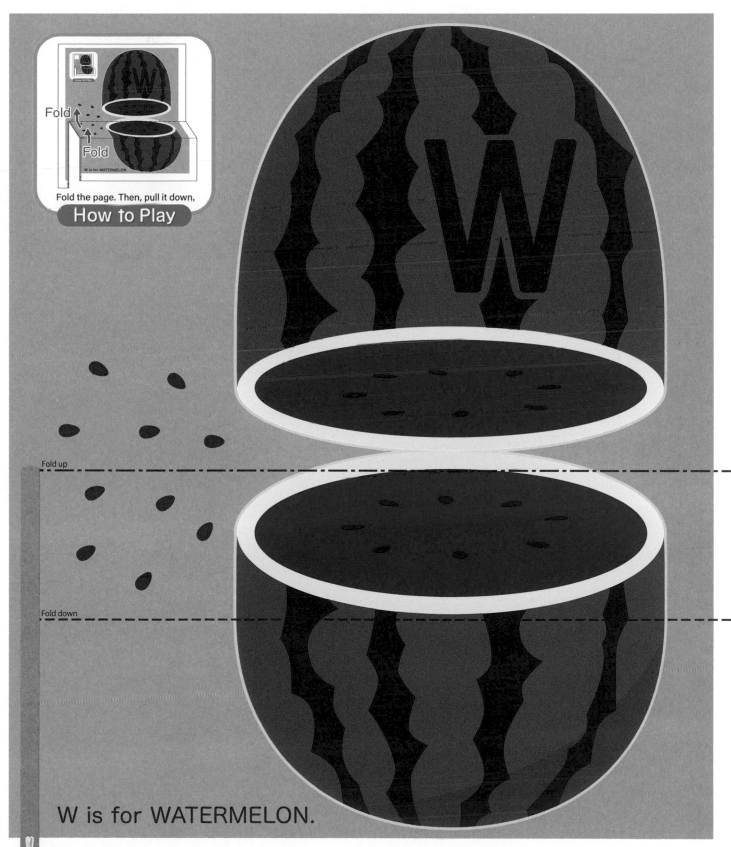

W is for WATERMELON.

Parents: Cut along the gray line for your child.

Sticker
Good job!

Trace the Letter X

  Trace the X and say "X."

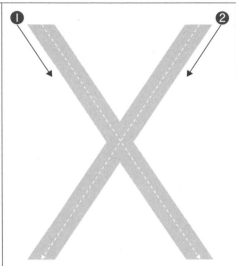

XYLOPHONE

FOX

 Color the FOX.

X is for FOX.

Find the Letter X

To Parents: Cut along the solid gray lines. Fold along the dotted lines to make mallets. Demonstrate how to play the xylophone, making sounds from low-pitched (for the longest bar) to high-pitched (for the shortest).

Play the xylophone with the mallets. Then, find the letter X.

Cut out the mallets. Fold
Fold down
Fold
Fold down
How to Play

X is for XYLOPHONE.

Parents: Cut out the mallets for your child.

Fold down   Fold down

Trace the Letter Y

To Parents: In this activity, your child will practice picking matching colors. Ask them to point to the purple yarn and color it purple. Then, ask them to point to the yellow yarn and color it yellow.

 Trace the Y and say "Y."

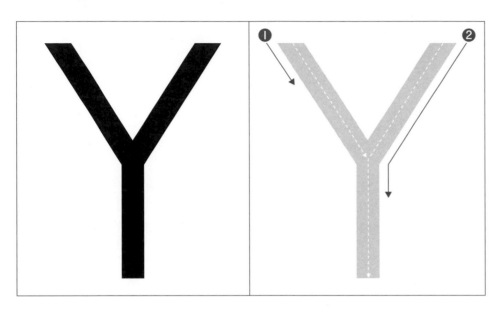

YACHT

YARN

 Color the YARNS.

Y is for YARN.

Find the Letter Y

To Parents: Here, your child will practice the line-drawing skills needed for proper handwriting. Guide your child to follow the gray dotted line with their finger. Then, have your child trace the line with a crayon.

  Find two versions of the letter Y in the picture. Then, trace the large Y.

Y is for YACHT.

Trace the Letter Z

To Parents: In this activity, your child will practice tracing straight lines. Ask them to use their pointer finger to trace the zebra's stripes. Then, let your child try with a black crayon.

  Trace the Z and say "Z."

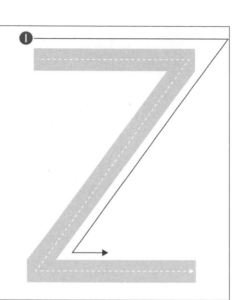

ZOO

ZEBRA

 Draw lines from ➡ to ➡.

Z is for ZEBRA.

Find the Letter Z

To Parents: Name each animal. Then, work on matching. Start with the *part*, then ask your child to point to the animal it's *part of*. Repeat this so your child can learn to make connections between parts and a whole more quickly.

 Draw a line from each *part* of an animal shown in a circle below to the *whole* animal it's *part of*. Trace the dotted gray lines of the Z, first with your finger, then with a crayon.

Z is for ZOO.

example

Let's Play with Alphabet Cards!

To Parents: There are countless ways to have fun and learn with alphabet cards. Start with using 5 or 6 cards and gradually increase the number of cards based on your child's progress.

  There are many ways to play with these cards. Have fun!

What's This?

① Shuffle 5 or 6 cards and put them in the envelope.
② Show part of the card and have your child guess the letter.

Pick Up a Card

Put a few cards on a table. Say the word that is featured on one of the cards. Let your child choose the card that matches that word.

What Begins with A?

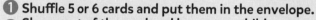

① First, show the letter side of the card to your child. Then, flip the card over and say "A is for apple." Ask them to repeat after you. Do the same for the next 5 or 6 cards.
② Show the letter side of the card again. Ask, "What word begins with this letter?" As your child answers or tries to remember, turn the card over and show the illustration. Repeat with the other cards.

Find the Cards

① Ask your child to close their eyes while you hide the cards in various places—be sure part of the card is visible.
② When you're ready, ask your child to open their eyes. Encourage your child to find the hidden cards.
③ Each time your child finds a card, ask them to say the letter or word on the card.

• Make a Card Case •

Find and cut out the card case on page 63.
Follow this diagram to fold it.

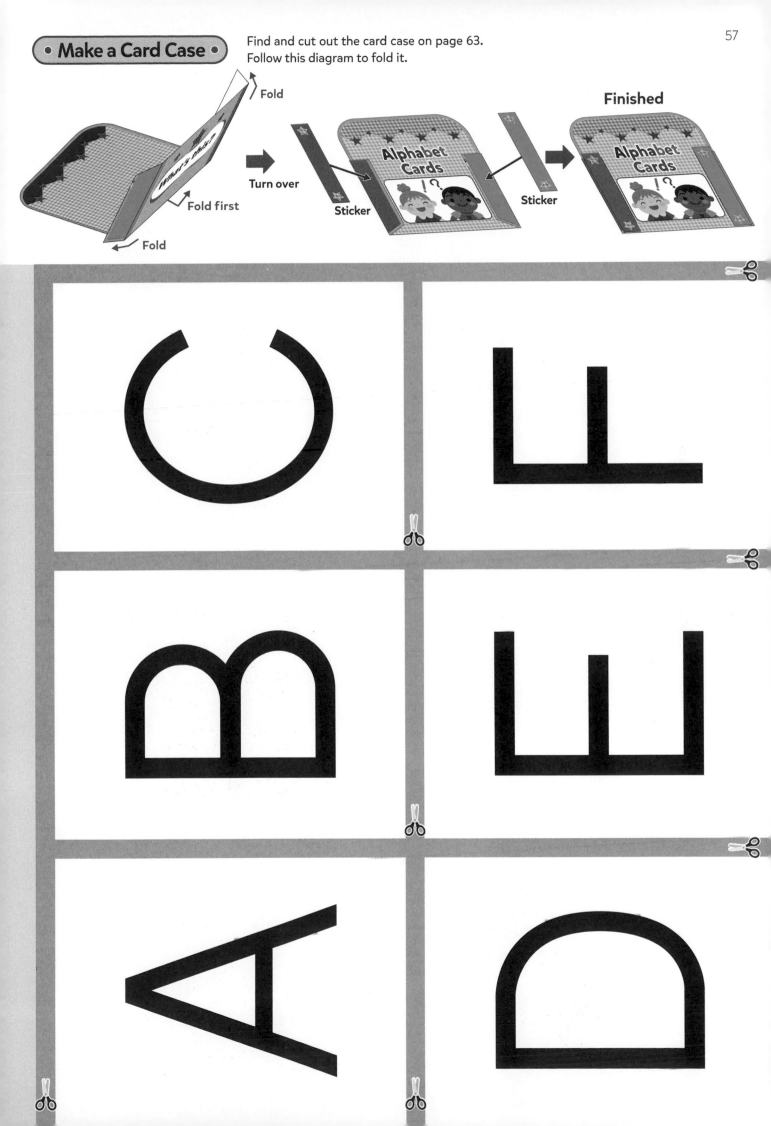

Fold

Fold first

Fold

Turn over

Sticker

What's this?

Alphabet Cards

Sticker

Finished

Alphabet Cards

Make Your Own Alphabet Cards

To Parents: Cut along the solid gray lines to create a deck of alphabet cards. Follow the gray lines to cut out the card holder on page 63 as well.

 Alphabet Cards

FROG

CAR

ELEPHANT

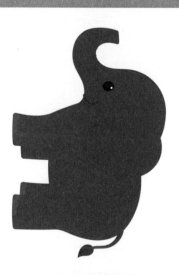

BEAR

DOG

APPLE

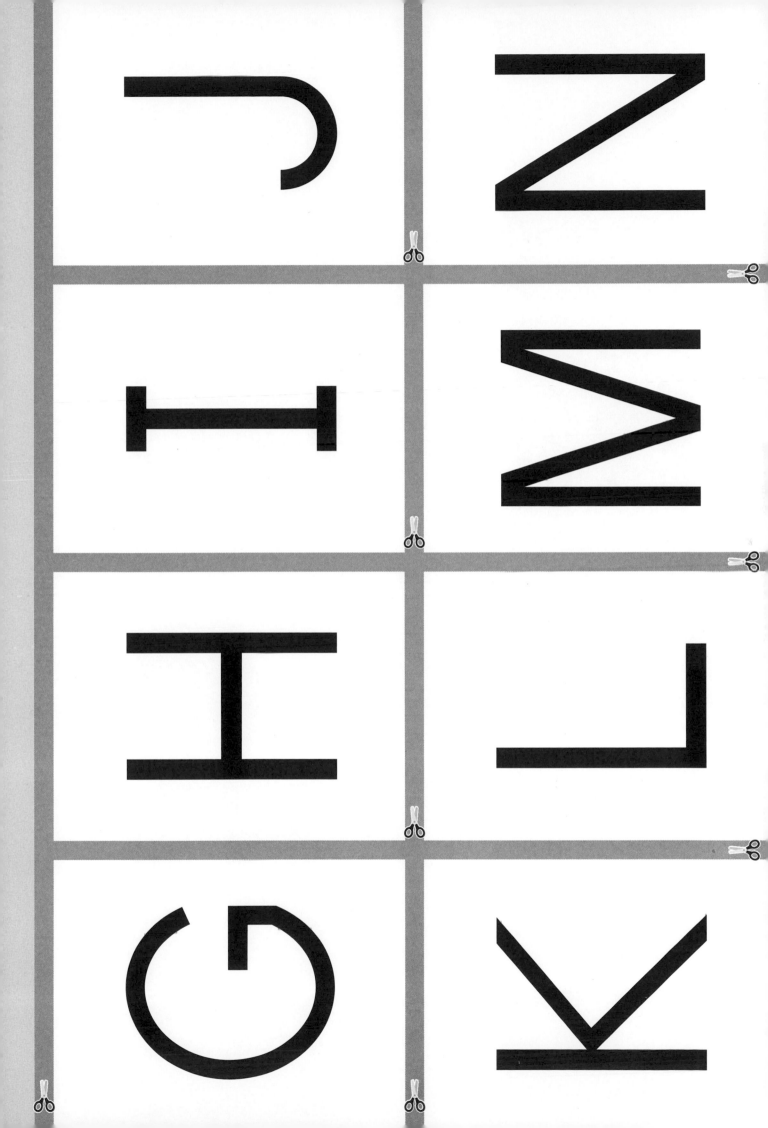

NIGHT

JAM

MONKEY

ICE CREAM

LION

HEART

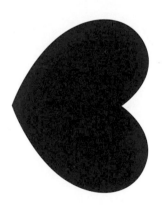

KOALA

GORILLA

VIOLIN

RABBIT

UNICORN

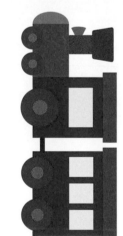

QUEEN

TRAIN

PIG

STAR

ORANGE

X

Z

W

Y

Alphabet Cards

What's this?

2

1

ZEBRA

XYLOPHONE

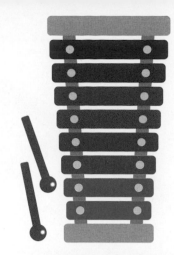

YACHT

WATERMELON

2

1

WIPE-CLEAN Alphabet Board

Let's write the letters by tracing the lines.

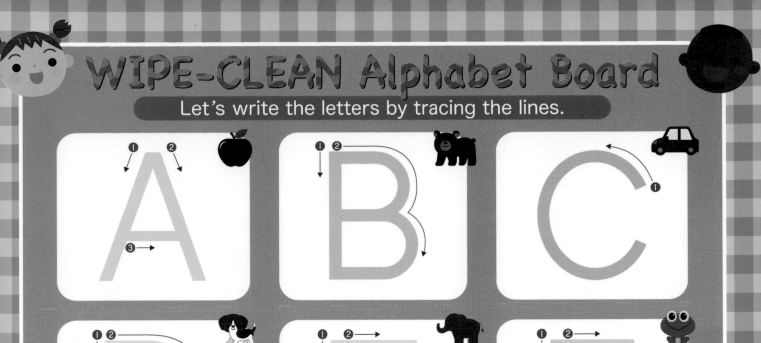

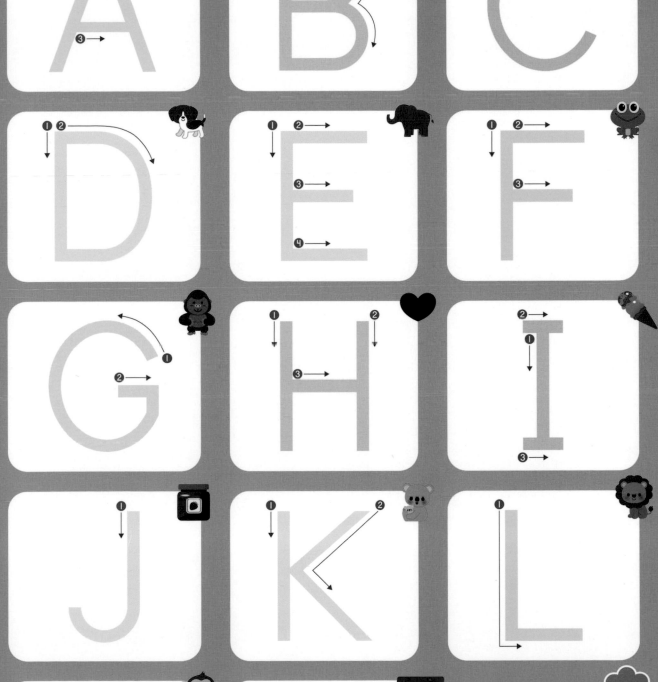

Use water-based markers on both sides of the board. When your child is finished writing, erase the board with a damp cloth or a tissue.

WIPE-CLEAN Alphabet Board

Let's write the letters by tracing the lines.

Practice writing your favorite letters.